Coloring Gifts™: Gifts of Friendship

An Adult Coloring Book Celebrating Friends

By Ligia Ortega
ColoringPress.com

This book is dedicated to Tina M. Thank you so much for being a true friend through it all for many years.

I also wanted to give a very special thanks to all the wonderful colorists who have colored my pages and shared their work. Thank you for all the love and encouragement you give.

Artist's Message

It means so much to me that you have chosen to purchase my book. Thank you from the bottom of my heart for your support of my work. I hope it brings you or a loved one hours of coloring pleasure, and that any gifts given from this book bring the recipient a tangible show of love and appreciation.

All images in this book were hand drawn by me. I then worked to digitize every page and assembled them electronically to prepare for printing. This coloring book has been a true labor of love, representing months of work (plus sleep deprivation, neglect of time with loved ones, and other work!). I took the time and additional expense to officially register this book with the Copyright Office. Please respect Copyright Law.

You may:

-Copy the uncolored pages on other paper preferences for yourself.
-Post colored images on social media.
-Give the colored pages as a gift.
-Use the physical colored pages for cards or bookmarks.
-Those cards and bookmarks may be given as gifts.
-Give a physical book you purchased as a gift.

You may not:

-Share physical or electronic copies of uncolored pages with anyone else, whether free or for sale.
-Post uncolored pages anywhere online, claim them as your own, or distribute uncolored pages via e-mail or electronic downloads.
-Incorporate uncolored or colored images on items besides colored pages, bookmarks, and cards.
-Sell uncolored or colored images, cards, or crafts made with the coloring pages, use them on products, or for any commercial usage.

Copyright © 2017 Ligia Ortega. All rights reserved. I am grateful for your support of artist/author's rights.

In accordance with the U.S. Copyright Act of 1976, the scanning, uploading, and electronic sharing of any part of this book without the permission of the artist/author constitutes unlawful **piracy** and **theft** of the artist/author's intellectual property except for the provisions above. Coloring any image does not transfer copyright or any rights to you, nor does it create a new copyright in your name. If you would like to use material from the book, prior written permission must be obtained by contacting the artist/author at:

ColoringGifts@yahoo.com   ColoringGifts.org   www.facebook.com/ColoringGifts

ISBN: 978-1974695706

ISBN: 1974695700

About This Book

In this day and age when so much of our communication is electronic, giving a colored page to someone as a gift would be a very special act indeed. I thought a book that had pages to be given as gifts would be unique and fun to make, so I set out to work on one – in the months that followed, I ended up with enough material for a series of twelve Coloring Gifts™ books! A Coloring Gifts™ book can be used in a variety of ways. This book can be given as a gift to celebrate friendship with someone who enjoys coloring. Colored pages can be gifted as is, framed, or made into cards or bookmarks using the instructions I have provided in the back of the book. The investment of time and creativity to color enhances the act of giving a gift of friendship and makes the Coloring Gift™ memorable to both giver and receiver.

There are many good reasons to celebrate friendship. Friendship has wonderful benefits. Friends help cheer us up when we are down, help us have a sense of belonging, boost happiness, and reduce stress. These psychological benefits translate into physical health as well: having good friends helps reduce risk of illness by lowering cholesterol, heart rate, and even blood pressure! Not to mention that spending time with friends is fun, and at times quite necessary for our sanity.

The act of coloring has been shown in scientific studies to give the same physical and mental benefits as deep meditation, and the theme of these coloring pages can be used to focus attention on the positive aspects of friendship and also in wishing someone you are friends with well. These coloring pages can also be used as a prayer or meditation aid. For those who pray and would like to focus on the spiritual aspects of friendship, I have added an appendix in the back of the book with scripture verses that focus on friendship to use alongside the book as you color. For those who meditate, this book, along with the act of coloring, can be used as part of Loving Kindness Meditation, which is also outlined in the appendix.

It is my wish that you enjoy coloring the pages of Coloring Gifts™ along with the physical and mental benefits friendship brings. I hope that the finished creations bring love and support to you or to someone in your life you want to offer a dose of affection and gratitude to. This is Volume 3 in the *Coloring Gifts™* series, and follows Volume 1, *Coloring Gifts™: Gifts of Thanks* and Volume 2, *Coloring Gifts™: Gifts of Encouragement*. I am already working on the next volume of *Coloring Gifts™* with yet more uplifting quotes to help you focus on the positive things in life. Please visit my site at ColoringGifts.org or find me on Facebook at facebook.com/ColoringGifts to share your colored pages, to get coloring tips, and for more ideas on how to use your colored pages as gifts.

Thank you from the bottom of my heart for choosing Coloring Gifts™ and I hope you enjoy the book!

Ligia Ortega

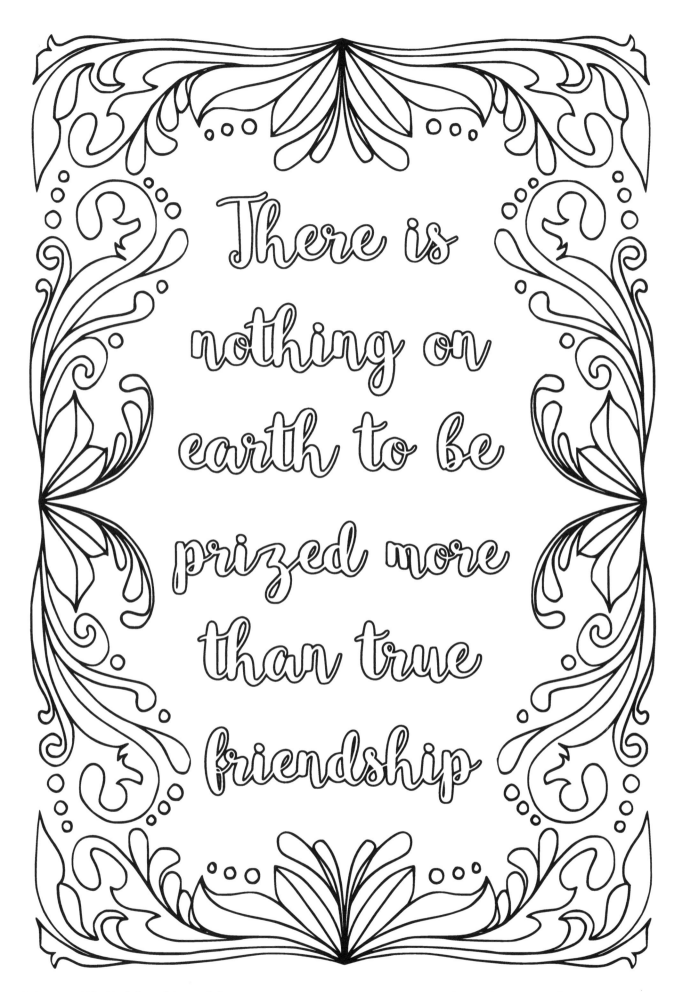

Friends? She's more like a sister

A day spent with a friend is a day well spent

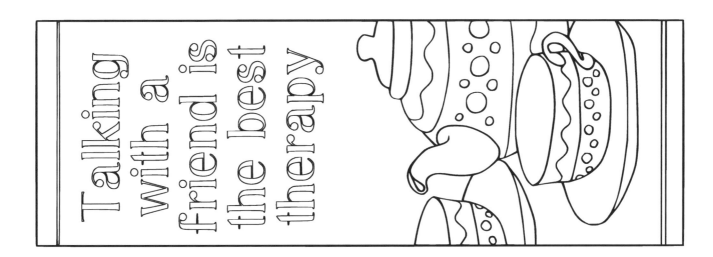

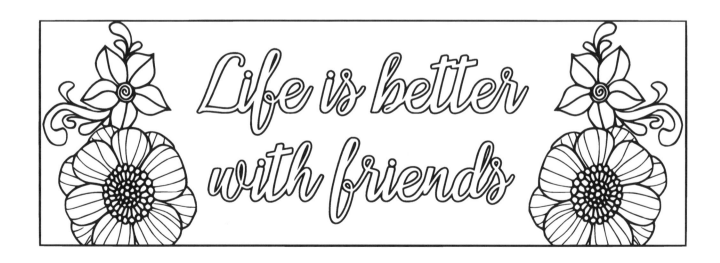

Bonus Pages

In addition to the Coloring Gifts ™ book series, I have been working on other coloring books for adults. The following coloring pages are from other books I have published under Coloring Press.

The first image is from Volume 1 of my Coloring Gifts ™ series, *Coloring Gifts: Gifts of Thanks*. The second image is from Volume 2, *Coloring Gifts: Gifts of Encouragement*.

The third image is from Volume 1 of my Vintage Grayscale Adult Coloring Book Series, *Arthur Rackham's Fairies and Nymphs*. The book has carefully curated and restored images from the work of one of my favorite vintage illustrators. I am already working on Volume 2 of this series. Visit ColoringPress.com for more information on grayscale coloring.

The remaining images are from my *Simple Kaleidoscopes* coloring books. I took on the challenge of making kaleidoscope images by hand rather than having software generated ones. It was fun watching them come to life from my own hand-drawn black and white coloring image. These kaleidoscopes are published as full size 8.5x11 books and also as a travel size book, *Pocket Kaleidoscopes*. Black background versions of these books are in the works too. I published these books in response to colorists asking for a less intricate kaleidoscope where they could show off their shading or just have larger spaces to color. Their bold lines and larger spaces also work well for people with low vision or issues with hand control. The travel size books are perfect for taking with you to the mechanic, the dentist, the doctor's office, or any place where you may have to wait. They make the time fly by quickly and the wait a lot more pleasant, and their small size means you can usually finish coloring a page in one sitting.

Pocket Kaleidoscopes - Regular and Black Background Books © Ligia Ortega - ColoringPress.com

Appendix

How to Add Special Touches to Your Coloring Gifts

Bible Verses About Friendship

Loving Kindness Meditation

How to Add Special Touches to Your Coloring Gifts™

The time spent in coloring your pieces is a gift to the recipient. The pages can be given as is, or with a letter to let the recipient know that you are grateful for their love and friendship. If you're looking to make your gift extra special, there are several things you could do to add some pretty touches to your Coloring Gifts™ pages. I have example photos and links to some basic supplies I mention below on my site, ColoringGifts.org, to help you find them easily.

You could frame the colored pages. Full size images are approximately 8x10 so they should fit either in an 8x10 frame or in a larger frame with a mat sized 8x10, or adhered on top of a coordinating larger page of colored or patterned paper to give it a more colorful background before being framed. This can be done with a glue stick or with a tape runner. The smaller pages can be framed, they are approximately 5x7 in size to fit a 5x7 frame or a larger frame matted to 5x7 or adhered to a background piece of paper and placed in a larger frame.

The smaller half size pages can also be used for cards. You can purchase blank cards in white, kraft, or bright colors, trim your design, and use a tape runner to attach the cut page to the card. Another idea is to buy colorful cardstock and score and fold it in half and attach the cut page to the card using a tape runner. Depending on how you would like to set up your cards you can go with 5.5x8.5 cards and use A9 envelopes or you could use 5x7 cards with A7 envelopes.

To make bookmarks, cut out your colored bookmark, add a layer of coordinating colored cardstock or pretty patterned paper that is slightly larger than the bookmark to give it a border and extra pizazz, and then you can laminate with self-laminating sheets. If you'd like to add more details, you could punch a hole on top of the bookmark and loop ribbon, yarn, or pretty string (maybe with beads or a small tassel) to add an extra special touch to your bookmarks.

Don't forget to share your creations with me on Facebook.com/ColoringGifts

I can't wait to see your finished pieces!

Bible Verses About Friendship

Ruth 1:16-17

2 Kings 2:2

Proverbs 11:14

Proverbs 17:17

Proverbs 18:24

Proverbs 19:20

Proverbs 27:5

Proverbs 27:17

Ecclesiastes 4:9-10

Luke 6:31

John 13:34-35

John 15:12-13

Romans 12:10

1 Corinthians 10:24

Ephesians 4:32

Colossians 3:14

1 Thessalonians 5:11

Hebrews 1:24

1 Peter 4:8

James 1:2-4

Loving-kindness Meditation

Loving-kindness meditation can be practiced at any level of intensity desired, but in its essence it is a heart meditation and should not be limited to sitting, formal meditation, but rather taken into the outside world at work, at home, and into everyday interactions and activities - such as coloring!

There are several different ways to practice Loving-kindness meditation:

Visualization - You can see a mental picture of the person you want to send loving kindness to and picture them feeling healthy and happy.

Thoughts – Focus your mind on an act of kindness or good qualities of someone you are thinking of.

Verbal – Repeat phrases. This is an effective way to focus our attention, examples are given below.

The way Loving-kindness meditation works is that it begins with directing loving kindness to yourself. Close your eyes and think about what you wish to have in life. Some examples are phrases such as, "May I be happy. May I be healthy. May I be filled with peace. May I be strong." If there is resistance to sending loving kindness to yourself, that means there is some inner work to be done to accept wishing yourself kindness before you can give loving kindness to others.

Once loving kindness can be given to oneself, then it can be developed toward others. Continue by sending loving kindness to someone who has helped you or offered you friendship. "May you be happy. May you be healthy. May you be filled with peace. May you be strong." This is a good step to help you focus on the person you are coloring a blank page for or someone you feel grateful for.

The next are optional steps to take if you would like to continue beyond the first person, you could visualize someone you feel neutral about. You may find this difficult to do because, in general, we tend to classify people as positive or negative in our lives.

A more advanced step is to continue to yet another person: someone you are having a difficult time with or you dislike. It can be empowering to send love to these people.

And the final step is to send loving kindness to the whole world: "May all be happy. May all be healthy. May all be filled with peace. May all be strong."

A recent study showed that people practicing this type of meditation several days a week for 15 minutes over nine weeks had a reduction in depressive symptoms and illness, and experienced an increase in life satisfaction and positive emotions.

I hope you enjoyed Coloring Gifts ™!

Please take a moment to leave a review on Coloring Gifts™'s Amazon book page.

For coloring tips, gift ideas, and to find Coloring Gifts ™ and my other books on Facebook, please visit:

ColoringPress.com

Made in the USA
Lexington, KY
09 September 2017